Adulterated
Pummeling success out of our kids

Josh Zepess

Lifesaver Leadership Development
www.LifesaverLD.org
Orlando, FL

Copyright © 2018 by Josh Zepess
Disclaimer: The material presented in this book is for informational purposes. While care has been taken to present the concepts in an accurate and updated fashion, the author makes no expressed or implied warranty of any kind and assumes no responsibility for errors or omissions. No liability is assumed for incidental or consequential damages in connection with or arising out of the use of the information contained here.

All rights reserved. No part of this book may be reproduced, stored in a special system, or transmitted, in any form or by any means, electronic, mechanical, photocopying, recording or otherwise without prior permission from the publisher.

Printed in the United States of America

First printing, 2018

Ordering Informaion
Special discounts are available for quanity purchases, associations, non-profits, and others. Please contact Lifesaver Leadership Development.
www.LifesaverLD.org

Library of Congress Cataloging
ISBN-13: 978-0-9997160-1-4

Table of Contents

1 An Old Hope

2 Get Real

3 Let's Coddle

4 Always A Day Away

5 Dukes up

6 Making The Grade

7 Dollars and sense

8 18th Place

9 Stranger Danger

10 Slap A Label

11 Line Up

12 Bad Copy

13 Childish Success

14 Give 'Em A Chance

Special thanks to the Zepess and Sirbu Families for a lifetime of support and laughs

To all those that believed in me For all those that can use some belief in themselves

"Children have the unforgiveable habit of growing up."

-- Bjarne Reuter

8

adulterate

verb adul·ter·ate \ ə-ˈdəl-tə-ˌrāt \

to corrupt, debase, or make impure by the addition of a foreign or inferior substance or element.
(Merriam-Webster)

1 AN OLd HOpe

We never stood a chance.

In a life that was meant to be great from the word go, we fell down the mountain of success to an average existence. That's right, we had it all. From Day One. Every characteristic for winning that was bestowed upon us by our creator was firmly planted in our new bodies. Perhaps it ran a bit wild and undisciplined, but it was there to show us the way to an amazing life.

Then it happened. From Day One. Instead of being guided in the ways of competence to handle our gifts, we were napalmed. Instead of being parented, we were befriended. Instead of being taught, we were marketed. Instead of being allowed to win, we were slipped every lesson on how to lose. It's not that we were convinced, rather that we were wore out. The type of mental conditioning that creates a truth from repetition. Of course, our truth needs no basis in reality; that is, until we're *faced* with reality.

Then, as we leave our two decade long training grounds of our parents' home, we fall flat on our face. The world laughs at us as we try to learn to stand and walk without our crutches, just the thing we've been training to do the entire time. Then we're free, or so we believe. The irony is that we've never been more subjugated, conditioned, and entrained than at this very moment. We are at the apex of our opportunity yet at the trough of our capability.

We may even have a confidence, or a swagger about us. We paid attention, we did well in school, and we managed to survive our parents not killing us for doing something dumb. Surely, we are now prepared to take on the world. Until we find out that we were trained in the wrong sport. We were taught how to follow instructions, but reality is requiring us to think. We were instructed to walk when the world is screaming at us to run. We proudly displayed our 18th place just like a winner, but Nature just fell off her perch in a fit of laughter at the mere suggestion. What the heck just happened?

It is said that it only takes 30 days to build a habit. What then, should we call it when we are subjected to 18 years of hand-me-down instruction, smarter-than-us marketing, and poor example? No doubt we have the habits. The question is whether or not they are serving us in life.

This is not about finding fault. There are reasons all around us as to why we struggle to find our purpose, get ahead financially, or just discover that elusive happiness. From parents who parrot, to marketers who mesmerize and distract, to a school system built around employee development, we have good examples of bad examples on understanding and capturing any of the above. At the end of the day, however, if we lose, does it really matter whose fault it is? Is their *mea culpa* going to take care of our family, provide us wealth and happiness, and give us the freedom to create a great life? Let's put the judgement aside and look towards the only thing we can change: Our future.

They say success leaves clues. Well those clues still lie in within us and they are no more evident than in our *unadulterated* children. We'll explore how we sap the success from their tree of life and we'll finish with a quick reminder of those attributes that were similarly robbed from us necessitating us to become a bit more childish. The first step to a new reality is awareness of our existing world. From there it then becomes our choice to recapture our youthful gifts or remain in an aging quandary

Yet what exactly is success? For our purposes, success is Freedom. Wouldn't you agree that if you had the means to do what you want, when you want to, and how you want to, that such a life would be considered successful? What exactly is Freedom? Freedom is the product of a sufficient quantity of three things:

Freedom = Time x Money x Identity

Lacking any of the three, we'll find Freedom difficult to obtain or maintain. If we have lots of money but no time, we may be a doctor, but we're not free. If we have lots of time and no money, we may be unemployed, but we're similarly not free. If we have both time and money but we haven't built the identity (self-worth) to have earned either, we won't have our freedom for long.

Look, if we're living the life we would otherwise design if we were billionaires, then God bless. We have achieved a level of Freedom that most will never experience. If we're living anything less than our truest desire, and there were a way to get there, what else should life be about other than the journey there?

It then begs the question, are we really raising our kids or are we lowering them into a tough life? Are we giving them a chance or dashing their hopes and dreams? In no way am I suggesting that we would ever intentionally hurt our kids, but what if we didn't even know were doing it? Could it be we "took the hook" first and just like faithful followers, we passed down the poison to our unsuspecting offspring?

There is a concept called the illusory truth effect. It states that if something is repeated enough times, it becomes true to us. In fact, the more it is repeated, the truer it becomes to us since familiarity breeds truth. Of course, no amount of repetition can make it more or less true in reality, but in our world, we might take it as gospel and forthwith preach it to our kids. We will certainly feel like we're doing the right thing but may be planting devastating seeds in our youth.

What are some of these things we say and do that may not be serving our kids to succeed in life? Welcome to the book. Enjoy it, think about it, disagree with it but please find as many nuggets as possible to create a thought, elicit a discussion, start a movement, or perhaps change one thing for the better in your own family.

Author's note: The "we" referred to throughout this book is not just us as parents. It's us as society, school, counselors, professional doctors, marketers and advertisers, and any other source of influence on us or our kids. There are more of us than you think.

EVERYTHING WE SEE IS A SHADOW CAST BY THAT WHICH WE DO NOT SEE.
MARTIN LUTHER KING, JR.

2 Get real

If you want to see me do something, tell me that I can't do it and get out of my way. I wasn't always like that though, erring on the side of caution and futility as a child. As our kids' number one influencer, we can be their biggest cheerleader or their most dangerous thief. We can root them on into the formerly impossible or we can ground them into a pointless realism. We can help them see a new future or we can blast them with the past. What if we allowed our kids to ask "What if?"

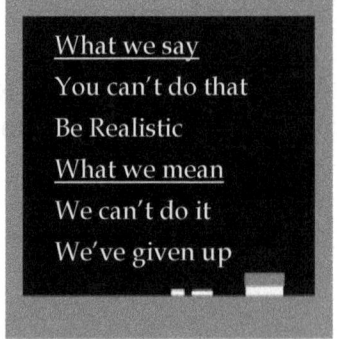

What we say
You can't do that
Be Realistic
What we mean
We can't do it
We've given up

Kids come to us with no limits and big dreams. When young, everything is possible. They can become astronauts, supermen, wonder women, and even presidents of the United States[1]. Then little by little, family, schools, and society start chipping away at the possibilities

---

[1] though some of the luster may be gone on that one

until we've honed them into good little soldiers just like everyone else. Then our kids grow up to *be* like everyone else, *do* like everyone else, and *have* like everyone else. But is that really what we'd call success?

WHERE THERE IS NO VISION, PEOPLE PERISH. PROVERBS 29:18

Their vision is clear and unobstructed, sometimes to the point where they go too far and hurt themselves. Of course, we should at least warn them of the danger if not stop them from doing something they will regret. It's when we exaggerate our caution into their field of view of a crazy (only by today's standards) future that we risk killing their dream and replacing it with the lead balloon of our reality. Who stole *our* dream? Who took *our* lollipop? Do you remember that day?

So we advise our kids to be a bit more realistic. After all, what if they fly too high and then have to take the fall back to earth? If we treat this metaphorical question as if it would physically kill them, we will never allow them to escape the gravitational pull of an average society.

What is realistic anyways? Isn't realism just a time-dependent excuse to give up? Electricity is not just realistic today, but an obvious staple of our daily lives. However, only a short 200 years ago, the candle industry wasn't too worried. Good thing Ben F. and later Thomas E. had a bit of unrealism in their vision. Flying in a heavier-than-air machine was crazy only 150 years ago, but thankfully Wilbur and Orville weren't being realistic, else they might have been shoemakers. Everything realistic that we enjoy today was at one time unreal.

 IF YOU BELIEVE YOU CAN OR CAN'T, YOU'RE RIGHT. HENRY FORD

Those with the vision to narrow that gap are the pioneers that have found a way to max out their life and build immense wealth. What if we encourage such vision in our kids and stop crapping on each idea that they create just because we can't fit it into our realistic view of the world? The most dangerous part of all of this is when <u>our</u> belief system rains down on them, like a venomous trickle. Belief is part of a cyclical process that can either create success or destroy it for our kids. Either way, it is an amazing predictor of the future. Henry Ford is famous for saying, "If you believe you can or can't, you're right."

Belief Cycle
Belief → Attitude → Behavior → Results

Here's how it works in a nutshell. If our kids believe they can do something, they will have a good attitude about it and feel good about doing it, which will lead to the right actions that cause the right results and a successful outcome. This, in turn, raises their belief that it can be done even higher and raises their expectations for the next time.

Unfortunately, the reverse holds just as true and is often the most experienced by all of us. For example, a child sees her family struggle with money and doesn't believe wealth is a possibility. She goes to school, but doesn't see the point in trying too hard. What's the use? It's not going to help. So with lackluster behavior, she naturally gets subpar grades.

Combined with her poor outlook and low expectations, her school results and eventual work performance keep her financially struggling for years. Her original belief is affirmed, further entrenching her bad attitude. Down the spiral she goes, eventually bringing her own kids with her.

The challenge is that belief in one area pervades in others. Given that the highest order belief is in themselves, if they struggle in one area, it can spill over into other areas. Our child above who was struggling with finance will probably have a tough time envisioning herself as an entrepreneur, happy spouse, or even a good employee. The low self-esteem brought on by her money woes becomes a limit to all possibilities as she sees it.

IF YOU WANT YOUR CHILDREN TO BE INTELLIGENT, READ THEM FAIRY TALES.
ALBERT EINSTEIN

What would happen if we replace "You can't" or "Be real" with "What if?" The latter question might be the greatest gift we can give to our kids for their vision. It gives them permission to dream, to create, and to explore. It allows them to see into an unscripted future where their dreams could one day become reality. This question also blocks realism and skepticism. Not that each of those don't have a place in the discussion, rather they belong further down the road as caution signs, not as a set of nail strips to flatten our tires before we make it twenty feet.

Imagine helping our kids aim for the moon and if they miss, they'll still land among the Stars. Let's pour on the belief, keep our personal and debilitating limitations close to our chest. Let's give them a chance….to dream in unreal ways, perform unreal feats, and to believe they can no matter what.

Raise our Kids

Take your kids' most passionate ideas, no matter how crazy, and have them write them all down. Frame it on their bedroom wall.

Then together choose one (or family vote) and have a brainstorm session on how you would do it if your lives depended on it. Get books, talk to experts and learn everything you can about it.

Write a business plan and take the first step. If that works, take the next step. Don't stop now.

Raise ourselves

Read
"Think and Grow Rich", by Napoleon Hill
   And
"The Secret", by Rhonda Byrne

3 Let's coddle

Kindness is one of our greatest qualities when used properly. Kids are born with it and practice it daily. There's nothing wrong and everything right with helping others, especially our kids, but what if we can go too far? What if too much help actually hurts?

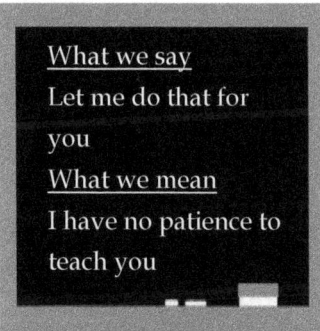

What we say
Let me do that for you
What we mean
I have no patience to teach you

There's a fine line between the two and like the proverbial "give a fish vs. teach to fish", could we be spending too much time giving and not enough time teaching? After all, nature isn't one to give much of anything except the opportunity to learn and do. If our kids don't learn in the safety of childhood, what do we suppose will happen when they must learn in the real world?

Parents are great teachers. Some better than others and some for better or for worse. Our pre-adulterated kids although amazing, are inexperienced and incompetent in life. So we take great pride in helping them learn the ropes from tying their shoes to walking to using a doorknob for the first time. The speed at which kids assimilate skills and information is truly incredible. Our societal instincts, though seemingly less so with other adults, can't stand to see children struggle. We want to jump in and teach if there's time, or just get it done if there's not. Keeping our kids "happy" and "struggle-free" seems to work well in the beginning.

Over time, our kids realize they effectively have, what is called in higher society, a butler and a maid. They poop, we clean. They cry, we coddle. They want, we give. It's not that we shouldn't be attentive to our young ones, especially when their only means of communication is not language, but what happens when we continue this trend as they become older? What principle of nature or life are they learning? When was the last time you sat and cried/complained and were immediately fed, given money, or got a raise at work?

 THE ONLY PLACE <u>SUCCESS</u> COMES BEFORE <u>WORK</u> IS IN THE DICTIONARY. V. LOMBARDI

It's when our propensity to give to our kids without regard to circumstance or effort, when taken to an extreme, eliminates all connection to reality. Nurturing the seed always comes before enjoying the fruit. The more we shield our kids to this connection, the more we spoil their ability to associate work with reward. The irony is that we're doing the work, just not getting the appreciation. Imagine helping our kids understand the work while giving them new appreciation and gratitude for not having to do it all.

We do what we can to help our kids avoid struggling. This sounds great on paper, but isn't it struggle where character, confidence, and self-esteem are born? Is it not *through* adversity where success hides?

All things in nature that are strong have struggled at some point. In fact, it is how nature works to build an ecosystem that won't fall apart at the first light breeze and drop of rain. Even a seed must develop roots and break ground before it can flourish. If it can't break ground or the necessary environmental (association) conditions aren't met, it will fail and die. If nature did not require this, that plant would not be able to handle the harsher conditions during its maturity and would cease to be a productive member of the ecosystem.

This principle is perfectly evident in that there are some things we just can't do for our kids. For example, they must learn to walk on their own. We can help a little, but ultimately they must figure it out. No amount of forcing them to their feet will help them walk better. They must fall many times as required by natural struggle but in the end, they will be stronger on their feet and more stable figuring it out on their own than if we were to keep propping them up and expect them to just stop falling down. Consider how many other things we do for them simply because we're able and not because it's in their best *long-term* interest.

I CRIED BECAUSE I HAD NO SHOES UNTIL I MET A MAN WHO HAD NO FEET.
HELLEN KELLER

This curt example is only amplified with we not only give, we give in to instant gratification. Clearly, we are the most guilty when it comes to instantly gratifying ourselves. Our spoiled kids are merely collateral damage. They manage to learn faster than we can even show them, but we still give our best.

We buy things we don't need, with money we don't have, so we can impress people we don't like, so we can be something we're not. We eat nutritionally poor because it's faster (no, it's not cheaper in any sense, but that's another discussion) and take drugs to quickly cure pain instead of working on the root cause of the stress of having too little wealth and health. We set the example of give me now and I'll see what I can do about paying later. This is just another abhorrent violation of the rules of nature. We can't pluck the fruit of success without planting and nurturing the seed of work.

Now we come to the real issue. This one issue could be the ultimate nail in the coffin for our kids and their ability to weather out the storm. Storms in life come and go and many are out of their control. It's up to our kids to survive them, which *is* fully in their command. The key to making it through is called toughness. In the animal kingdom, there is a lot of physical toughness required. In our comfortable world, the biggest difference between winners and losers is their mental toughness.

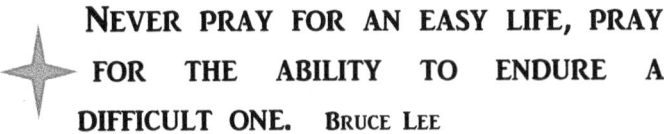

NEVER PRAY FOR AN EASY LIFE, PRAY FOR THE ABILITY TO ENDURE A DIFFICULT ONE. BRUCE LEE

Most good folks in our society have the mental toughness of a wet napkin. Our kids, following suit, are now struggling to adapt to a tough world where adversity strikes at will, we can't seem to have a social discourse on a topic that might offend someone, and where quitting is the soup d'jour...every day. By the way, it's okay that the world isn't all rainbows and unicorns. What's important is that when it starts raining, they have a strong umbrella, a raincoat to protect them, or the knowledge that they won't actually melt if they get wet. It's only a matter of *how* to endure until it passes. And it always passes.

Mental toughness must be built from the inside, just like learning to walk. It cannot be given, gifted, inherited, or otherwise transferred without cost. For our kids to develop this attribute, they must pay the price in full and up front. It's a hard lesson, but how valuable would it be to our kids, upon shooting for the stars in search of their dreams, to break through social, economic, and political barriers, build a staircase to the heavens, and grab their dream by the ascot? Okay, that may be too much, but how about at least not give up the first time someone hurts their feelings?

Am I suggesting any sort of cruelty to kids? Should we abandon them at a time of need? Absolutely not. While not giving in to every whim of a child may seem cruel on the surface, imagine the cruelty of coddling and protecting them from struggle only to find that they can never stand on their own in life, fully dependent upon the charity of us and society. And then when society says a naughty word, they fall to pieces. How exactly is that being nice? Consider the level of deceit required to allow them to grow up in a world that doesn't exist. Let's give them a chance to struggle, grow, and become the person worthy of greatness in an amazing world.

Raise our Kids

When your kids are old enough to speak, they are old enough to have responsibility. What better time than while young to introduce them to the concept of work-reward.

There are countless resources for chore ideas, with most starting at age 2. This is not an opportunity to slave-drive, rather make an agreement to reward for work. The rest is up to them.

Raise ourselves

Read
"177 Mental Toughness Secrets of the World Class", by Steve Siebold
And
"Grow a pair", by Larry Winget

4 ALWayS a day aWay

Kids are always in a rush. They don't know that they're supposed to slow down and save energy for later. More importantly, until they learn from us, they don't even know their energy is limited. They are so excited by life and for life that they want to pack it all in as if they might leave this world tomorrow. And then we come home from work, too tired to interact with them and we kindly inform them to stop being so full of life. We don't say it in so many words, but the meaning is clear. Take it easy. What worth having in life is easy and where exactly should they take it?

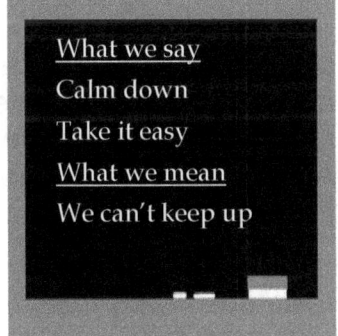

What we say
Calm down
Take it easy
What we mean
We can't keep up

Einstein noted that energy can neither be created nor destroyed, but he never claimed that it was limited with respect to our world. It would be akin to filling a small pail with sand and worrying about running out of sand on the planet. He did say that everything is energy, including us. What if kids feel the truth of this innately? And they operate on this principle accordingly, that is, until we force them to slow down, get into bed, stand in line, and just cool it off. It doesn't take long before that fire dims to only a few glowing embers. Eventually, our kids forget there was even a fire there to begin with and they learn how to be tired, stressed, and become the exhausted adults we know and love.

What is tired anyways? Is it really lack of energy or just lack of interest and excitement? If we thought back to our last exciting vacation, what were the chances that we were too tired to make it to the airport on time? I'm guessing somewhere between zero and none.

So we don't develop a lack of energy from getting older, we just lose our ambition, goals, purpose, and excitement about life. We forfeit every good reason we ever had for waking up in the morning. At what point did we give up on the dream and find excuses to wear out?

THE TWO MOST IMPORTANT DAYS OF YOUR LIFE ARE THE DAY YOU ARE BORN AND THE DAY YOU FIGURE OUT WHY. Mark Twain

Fortunately, kids are born with such an amazing outlook on life that they see no reason to have limited energy. Moreover, all those characteristics we wish to see in our children take energy. Creativity, concentration, cognition, just to name a few, take immense amounts of mental energy. We often ask our kids to use that mental energy while constraining their physical energy (isn't this called school?), yet the challenge may be ensuring our kids do not confuse the two. How many times must they hear 'take it easy', 'relax', 'slow it down', before they learn to be lackadaisical in all ways?

The concept of time as we know it was created by us. Not whether time exists, rather that we're trained to work 40 hours per week and take weekends off to 'rejuvenate' We learn to sleep at night, work during the day except during breaks, and repeat this process indefinitely until we expire or get fired. Did we not set our own trap?

Yet there are a few of us that are extremely wealthy, happy, and successful with the same twenty-four hours as those that struggle every day to make a living. How can that be? Perhaps some of us aren't playing by the arbitrary rules of time! Again, what example are we setting for our kids? Are we winding them up on society's clock or permitting them all the hours with which they were born?

 TOMORROW IS *ALWAYS* A DAY AWAY, ANNIE.

Once we do get our kids on a schedule, we often find ourselves quashing their sense of urgency. If they don't get to it today, since tomorrow will likely be a repeat, why not just do it then? What's the rush? This works in theory until the realization that tomorrow never comes. Consider how violating this rule works in life and business. We may teach that good things come to those who wait, it's the early bird that gets the worm (or at least the first shot at it, which is usually good enough).

Having a sense of urgency also compresses time. It can make an hour seem like a day, but with results of the latter. In a world that is increasingly focused on results, imagine getting more done in less time. Putting aside that we tell ourselves how we don't have time or are too tired, imagine taking a week's worth of work and getting it done by Tuesday. What would we do with the remaining three days? Could we write an opera, read a book, build a business, take martial arts classes, or perhaps have a meaningful conversation with our children?

Thomas Edison, in search of the electric light, hired a bunch of 'muckers' to help design and test each attempt so that he could fail faster. He knew that success was found through failure and that the faster he could fail, the sooner he would succeed. Imagine how unbounded our kids' success could be with an unbounded amount of time through urgency?

It's when we don't have a sense of urgency that we create a future emergency.

It's when we don't have a sense of urgency that everything becomes an emergency. We get behind the 8-ball, enter a reactionary mode, and like trying to tread water in rough seas, we eventually drown in the melee. Urgency is the breeding ground to proactivity, since there's plenty of time to with which, prepare. The alternative of slowing down or taking it easy is to react as needed and never quite get ahead.

In our attempt to have a little bit of peace and quiet from a rough day of meetings and beatings, we can inadvertently be turning off the energy and fire our kids rely upon to fuel their dreams. We must take care not to burn them out before they have a chance to light up the world. Let's give them a chance...to run fast, fail faster, and create more energy than we consume.

Raise our Kids

Have your kid interview three successful business owners in your town. Most truly successful folks will be gracious to any curious child, plus what a great school report it would make!

Use the following questions as a guideline to learn about how successful people think and do.
- What's your daily schedule like?
- What was your biggest struggle growing yourself and your business?
- What's been your greatest success so far?
- What's your vision for the next 10 years?
- What advice would you give to a kid my age to be successful in life?

Raise ourselves

Read
"Go for No", by Richard Fenton
And
"Essentialism", by Greg McKeown

 Dukes Up

Surely we don't want our kids hurting themselves or anyone else. But while physical fighting may not be tolerable (though it would only take one good shot on a bully for them to cower away and never bully anyone again), we must be careful that the lesson doesn't spill over into fighting for other things more important, like their life, career, family, and what's right. The alternatives to fighting are backing up or laying down, neither of which are historical launching points towards success. Life is going to be a battle for them and it will take competitiveness, mental toughness, and perseverance to make it up the hill. Are we preparing our kids for war or coddling them from the inevitable?

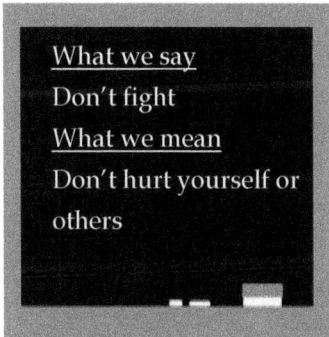

What we say
Don't fight
What we mean
Don't hurt yourself or others

There's a major difference between fighting *for* something and fighting *against* it. Fighting for something worthwhile is how we achieve and accomplish that which is greater than ourselves. It is a positive state of mind that can yield positive results if it's earned. Our natural instinct from birth is to fight for life, for freedom, and for others. Fighting against something often puts us in a destructive state of mind in which it doesn't matter if we lose as long as our foe loses too. It's all about the other person losing. There is enough of this type of fighting in the world and this is not the type of fighting that our kids are missing.

 YOU GET IN LIFE WHAT YOU HAVE THE COURAGE TO ASK FOR. OPRAH WINFREY

Nonetheless, our kids come with a level of fight in them that is often expressed as competitiveness. They compete to be first in line, to win a sports, or to have the most toys (the 'mine' syndrome). Sometimes competition is shunned by parents or school as creating winners and losers, but this is an essential lesson that must be learned in their formidable years. Winners raise their belief level and self-identity allowing them to continue creating bigger and better. Losers have the golden opportunity to learn and grow into better people and become winners. In fact, the only difference between a winner and a loser, with a positive competitive attitude, is time. Any child willing to put in the effort to develop their skills and put in the work will eventually win.

Furthermore, competition drives performance. Especially prior to adulteration, anytime a bar is set our kids often have the inclination to try to beat it. Here's the key: winning is a relative feat. Is a million dollars a lot of money? Compared to the dollar in our pocket, yes. Compared to the average net worth of the Forbes 400 list, heck no. Without a bar with which to measure themselves and the competitive spirit to climb it, performance not only wanes, it gets obliterated, along with any chance to win in life.

What's unfortunate is that many of us adults have lost our competitive spirit. The ones that do have it are often labeled greedy by the ones that don't, rationalizing that winning isn't everything.

WINNING ISN'T EVERYTHING. IT'S THE ONLY THING. "RED" SANDERS

On the surface it may seem selfish, but if we consider the life that winners create for their family, what can more unselfish? Naturally, the alternative is to shirk away as an average person living an average life. That might seem okay until our family needs us to win and we're left unprepared mentally, physically, and financially.

And If we do have any competitive spirit left, it's often channeled vicariously through our kids (ever see a little league game?) to the point where we not only lose our temper, but lose our self-respect in the hypocrisy of our sideline antics.

What if adults don't compete because we don't believe we can win anymore? Our pessimism about the life we created is that heavy weight on our lap that keeps us glued to our seats. Kids, however, have such a sense of optimism that they expect to win every time. Expectation, while not sufficient, is certainly a necessary condition for success. What if we can leave our kids with their high hopes instead of hitting them upside the head with our realism?

External competition, while extremely beneficial, is still a lower-order concept compared to internal competition. What if we can hone our kids' competitiveness towards others and direct it back at themselves? Isn't our truest purpose in life to become the best version of us? Is there any more that anyone can ask of us? The highest level of the competitive spirit is beating the person we were yesterday. Our kids, while young, learn at an amazing rate until we begin to overpraise for under-delivering, satiating them to the point where they stop growing. The true blessing our kids have is the ability to continue to grow. Of course we love them just the way they are. We just forget to finish that phrase with, "but I love you too much to allow you to stay where you are."

If we can allow our kids to compete and perform, we can help them avoid the dreaded disease of pansy-itis. Pansy-itis, in my opinion, is the leading cause of human failure today. It's the inability to talk about hard issues for fear of insult or judgement. It's not wanting to get into the ring for fear of being punched in the nose. It's the comfort zone, giving only the illusion of comfort, until life rocks the boat, without knowing how to swim. As adults, we all know that it's not *if* life happens but *when* it does, how *bad* it gets, and how *prepared* we are (or not). It's only known cure is the development of mental toughness.

I HATED EVERY MINUTE OF TRAINING BUT I SAID, "DON'T QUIT, SUFFER NOW, AND LIVE THE REST OF YOUR LIFE AS A CHAMPION." MUHAMMAD ALI

Mental toughness is the ability to withstand all that life throws at us. When life bullies our kids, how do they respond? Do they run away and expect that life won't follow them to the next town or do they stand and fight, realizing that the adversary's main gig is fear and confusion, neither of which are real? When we tell them not to fight, other than run or lay down, what other options are we proposing?

Look, everyone has their own adversary. All adversaries have a commonality though. They show up either right at the beginning of an effort (to squash it in its inception) or just before the big success at the end (last desperate attempt to stop us). Most successful people will tell you that just before they had their big breakthrough, all hell broke loose. It's the ones that can keep it together that make it to the top. Nowadays, though, most people, including kids being adulterated early, don't have the mental toughness required to win. Forget about persevering through rejection during an economic downturn under a communist regime, we can't make it past a stranger's unfounded and unimportant opinion of our new shoes.

It's not that our kids don't come with the perseverance though. Have we ever seen a kid ask incessantly for a cookie? There's no stopping them. Their will and mental toughness is off the charts and they're relentless until they get one. Of course we give in, not having a fraction of their perseverance anymore. Still we manage to wear them down over the years to stop asking questions, stop believing they can do it, and stop expecting to win. And it works like a charm, doesn't it?

Mustn't we fight for what we want in life? Few things in life, worth having that is, are given to us. Success rarely (actually, never, but that's a bigger discussion) falls in our lap. Telling our kids not to fight is like telling a baby cow to get into the veal box. It's cruel on every level.

> I ALWAYS FELT THAT MY GREATEST ASSET WAS NOT MY PHYSICAL ABILITY. IT WAS MY MENTAL ABILITY. BRUCE JENNER

So that begs the question, who do your kids idolize? Is it a sports star, movie star, musical artist, or is it mommy and daddy? Looking at the social media version of their "posters on the wall", it would seem the latter is quite rare. Why is that? Could it be that mommy and daddy aren't in the ring? That they're no longer fighting for anything?

Perhaps we're struggling for a paycheck but we're not fighting to win. Nobody cheers for spectators (save the one that streaks nude on the field), and our kids are looking to us to tell them whether to play or cheer for others. Let's give them a chance….to fight for what they believe in and for a life worth living.

Raise our Kids

Challenge them to take on a sport (physical or mental). From chess to football, swimming to martial arts. Inspire them to a victory by being involved directly through coaching or even participating. Make a pact to not quit before winning, no matter how tough it gets. Have a real reward for winning: family trip, big ticket item, etc.

Raise ourselves

Read
"Relentless", by Tim Grover
 And
"Be obsessed or be average", by Grant Cardone

6 Making the grade

Keep your penny for your thoughts, just give me two cents for every time I've heard this growing up. *Go to school, get good grades, get a safe and secure job, and success is yours.* Perhaps there

> What we say
> Get good grades
> What we mean
> Be more successful than us (money doesn't hurt either)

was a day when this was true, but is it the case anymore? We are in an age where grades are more important than learning, we teach how to pass a test instead of teaching how to think, and where even getting the grades doesn't guarantee anything close to success anymore.

What is the purpose of school? Is it to receive an education or to get good grades? I would guess that most parents would want their kids to get an education. After all, it's the skills and knowledge from education that provides our kids the competence to succeed at any career. Granted, we need a measuring stick to determine the competence of our children as they move on to the next level, but somehow we short-circuited the system and began to focus on them getting the grade, not on them attaining the competence in a skill that is supposed to produce such a grade.

I NEVER LET SCHOOLING INTERFERE WITH MY EDUCATION. MARK TWAIN

When we focus on learning, we find that good grades are the natural consequence of a higher level of competence. When we focus on grades, however, we find our ingenious kids looking for any way to get the grade, with competence relegated to a potential side effect. As we've legislated ourselves into a similar system for teacher accountability, we've successfully incentivized teachers to 'make the grade' first, then teach with the time and energy left over. Much like our personal budgets, there's not much left over at the end of the month.

The biggest beating, though, is yet to come. After all the focus on their grades with the late nights cramming mostly useless information into their heads, they finally achieve their diploma so that they can do it all over again at the college level. This time, however, it will cost them dearly. Their solid lessons into how to get a good grade in primary school is challenged a bit more with higher standards for performance. Moreover, the pressure of performance lies mostly with themselves helping the stress levels to rise almost as fast as their tuition bill[2].

Now the focus shifts to getting the degree, as if the degree was the golden ticket to an unlimited supply of (chocolatey?) success. The challenge deepens when our kids realize that everyone else was doing the same thing too[3]. Now it's a race to get a job in their field of study, which in itself is a longer shot than we may expect, with only 27% of people working in their field of study[4]. The lucky ones get the interview, the competent ones that learned and applied their knowledge along the way, get to stay.

This is no denouncement of college. What a fantastic place that allows for learning and growing. If college is the vehicle to get them where they want to go, don't let the door hit them in the butt. Or perhaps it's a trade school or entrepreneurship – if these are even discussed as options anymore.

---

[2] These are not without correlation

[3] Common wisdom, while not particularly wise, is certainly common

[4] Plumer, Brad. Washinton Post. May 2013

The irony is that the push for grades and degrees has become such a mantra that they forget *why* they are pursuing these things. Even worse, after so much conditioning, they will go to school to *figure out what they want to do!* That may be one very expensive lesson in how to start life in the hole, especially considering the opportunity cost of time and the financial cost of the tuition plus interest from any loans.

IF YOU ARE NOT WILLING TO LEARN, NO ONE CAN HELP YOU. IF YOU ARE DETERMINED TO LEARN, NO ONE CAN STOP YOU. ZIG ZIGLAR

Now our kids are fully adulterated and ready (or not) for their careers. Remember the days when there was loyalty between an employer and employee, with the latter helping the former during their productive years with the promise and fulfillment of the lifetime pension and gold watch? Me neither, but I've heard of those days and it's becoming more apparent that times have changed. Now they're in a workplace where even as a W-2 employee, they must consider themselves as independent contractors, or essentially self-employed. During our 18 years of training them on how to take directions and get a good grade, did we ever teach them how to think, be proactive, and develop the skills to succeed? Are they worthy of success?

Let us not forget what happens outside of work. Having focused on the grade (end result) at any cost, we see an interesting manifestation of this in their personal lives. This message carries over to the principal of looking good before being good. It's like keeping up with the Joneses' and their 4000 sq. ft. house, 3 cars, 2.5 cats and host of watercraft that they sporadically use. Yes, the Joneses' are over-leveraged and are one tiny emergency away from bankruptcy, but it sure looks good at the moment. It's the social equivalent of that piece of paper, called a degree, that has no inherent value but perhaps got them the job that doesn't pay them enough to have the life they desire.

And even if everything goes sparkling perfect - perfect grades, useful degree, and wonderful job - how exactly do grades correlate with success? After schooling them on how to survive in Corporate America, what happens when they are laid off, downsized, right-sized, or outsourced and must start over at 35, 45, 55, and then 65 years old? On average, people have 12 jobs between ages 18 and 48[5]. What happens when they find out their 401(k) can't retire them like pensions used to retire our parents?

---

[5] U.S. Bureau of Labor Statistics

LEARNING NEVER EXHAUSTS THE MIND.
LEONARDO DA VINCI

As a final consideration, what are we teaching our kids in school anyways? How is it that we spend time teaching them about the mating rituals of the horned frog, but not how to cook it? They learn a new dumb way to do simple math, but not how money truly works for them or against them. We give them condoms to put on bananas but don't teach the golden rule of respecting others. For what in life are we preparing them?

Imagine a focus on learning and education and letting the grades fall where they may. There are a host of amazingly successful of people (in terms of Freedom) that not only got poor grades, but dropped out of school altogether. But they were still voracious learners and students of life.

What if we can help our kids extrapolate the principles of hard work, focused learning, and mental toughness from education and into their entire life? Success then becomes a mirror of their true worth and not just another facade destined to blow away during the first rainstorm. Let's give our kids a chance...to truly learn and grow, and create so much inherent value that they're never without means.

Raise our Kids

Take one topic below per week/month that schools no longer focus on and teach these incredibly important life skills to your child (of course, you may have to learn them first):

- How money *really* works
- Home and Car – Buying/Selling and Management
- Building relationships – Marriage and Family
- Credit Cards and interest
- Integrity, Likeability, and Etiquette
- Cooking and other home skills
- Time Management
- Survival Skills outside of society
- Entrepreneurial mindset

Raise ourselves

Read
"As a Man Thinketh", by James Allen
And
"7 Habits of Highly Effective People", by Stephen Covey

 Dollars and Sense

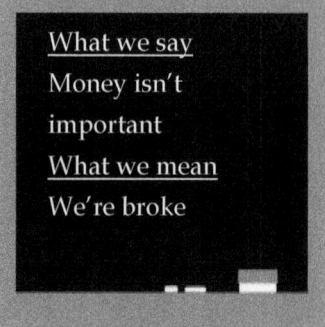

What we say
Money isn't important
What we mean
We're broke

It's more than interesting how our money stresses (caused by our mentality of money) manifest themselves so quickly in our kids. Make no mistake, nobody has a money problem. Money is only the effect of a cause, namely our beliefs about money that determine our actions therein. What if the money mindset (myths) that we pass onto our kids is the primary reason they will misunderstand, misuse, and stress about money until the day they die?

We must agree upfront that money is the lifeblood of our society. That without it, we're essentially dead. So having it offers more freedom than not having it. Let's look at a series of beliefs about money that we tend to repeat ad infinitum, training ourselves and our kids, like the blind leading the blind. These beliefs may or may not be true. Their veracity is not the point. Facts are certainly important when making financial decisions based on numbers, but when discussing the mindset of money, the question is whether these beliefs serve us or not to be in a better financial situation. If they serve us, believe away. If they don't, perhaps it's worth changing the script.

IF YOU WANT TO MAKE A MILLION DOLLARS, YOU MUST FIRST BECOME A MILLIONAIRE.

Money isn't everything.
Of course it isn't, but again, not the point. Oxygen isn't everything either, but you sure better have some to do *anything* else, right? By the way, when do you usually hear someone say this? Right after they lose a bunch of money or don't have anymore? It's that rationalization that helps them sleep at night. That should be our first clue. Money does, however, open up some doors that could lead to everything else. This mindset tends to lead us to treating money poorly, almost like nothing. Did you know that money goes where it's loved? If we don't respect it, it won't be hanging around us. If we were treated like nothing, would we hang around either?

Money isn't important
True or not, how is this serving us to attain more? Consider that most people are spending 2000 hours per year (or more) away from their family, friends, and passions to make money that they can then spend on their family, hobbies, and a bunch of things don't make them happy anyways.

How do your kids reconcile that when you get home after 10 hours of work and traffic and are pissed off and worn out? Anyone who believes this money myth probably has not given any away. Give away a few dollars to a homeless vet, a children's hospital, or just a friend in need, look into their eyes if you can, and tell me how unimportant money is.

Money can't make you happy
Here's one of my all-time favorites. Of course money cannot make you happy. Then again, neither can poverty. Can we just agree that money has little to do with happiness? Happiness is simply a choice.

So if we choose to be happy, do we want to be happy *with* money or *without* money? Imagine helping our kids understand that they can be happy...and have large sums of money. We would be giving them the best of both worlds instead of damning one world for the sake of the other. The irony is that the world of money which we damn is what often affords us the opportunity to do those things that make us happy.

Money is the root of all evil.
This aberration of the Bible could be the top reason why good people suffer in poverty. First, it doesn't say this - see Timothy 6:10. It says that the *love* of money is the root of all evil. If our focus is solely on the money and not on what good we can do with the money, then we're in certainly in trouble.

For what it's worth, if money and all that which is associated is so evil, why do our religious institutions ask for so much of it? Isn't money just a tool? Like a knife, it could surgically save our life or tragically take it. Imagine our kids understanding this simple concept. That not only are they not a slave to money, but they have a responsibility to handle it with the respect and care it deserves.

> **I NEVER WANTED TO BE RICH, JUST COMFORTABLE. THEN I FOUND OUT TO BE COMFORTABLE, I HAD TO BE RICH.**
> LES BROWN

There are a host of other money myths that we promulgate to our friends, family, and especially our kids. But even beyond what we say is how we handle money ourselves. If we consider that 45% of Americans have zero dollars in any form of retirement account, 46% could not find $400 for an emergency, and wages have not risen, inflation adjusted, in 40 years, what kind of example are we setting for them? What our kids *see* about our financial situation has lasting effects on their view of money. If they see stress, fighting, worry, fear, and depression from a lack of money, how could they possibly form a positive view of our societal lifeblood?

Like trying to win at a sport, it is important to know the rules of the game and have practiced the skills required to achieve a level of competence to win. In a game we all must play called LIFE, a big part of which deals with money, how can our kids ever expect to win when schools aren't teaching the basics of it, parents don't know it and it shows, and the financial industry's profits are proportional to their ignorance of it?

The good news is that the rules are simple. With discipline and effort, they can indeed win the game. Let's give them a chance...to understand money, appreciate money, and have all they desire of it.

Raise our Kids

Teach kids the bucket principle. One bucket is for savings, one bucket is for gratitude, and one bucket is for spending. The first two buckets get filled first, with 10-20% of any money they make into each and the rest goes into the spending bucket. Have them start making money as young as possible – mow lawns, sell lemonade. Give them an allowance for helping out if need be.

There should be a goal for the savings bucket (a big ticket item they really want) and a goal for the gratitude bucket (have them pick a charity.) Each month, track progress on the savings goal until there's enough money to buy it. Give away the gratitude money to someone in need (not to you, no matter how late the mortgage payment is!).

Raise ourselves

Read
"Cash Flow Quadrant", by Robert Kyosaki
And
"Secrets of the Millionaire Mind", by T. Harv Eker

8 18ᵗʰ place

There are no 18th place trophies in nature. We can sugar coat it, we can pretend like it, we can even put some lipstick on it, but it won't make it an easier when our adulterated children face the real world. If you can read this book (8th grade level), you probably already know that life isn't all sunshine and rainbows. That nature has rules and standards and there is no violating them. We can hope it isn't so, or we can prepare our kids to handle it. Either way, nature will hold them accountable.

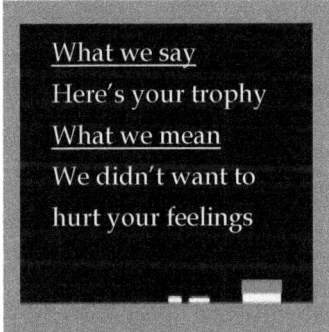

What we say
Here's your trophy
What we mean
We didn't want to hurt your feelings

The beat down here comes in several flavors. As we disconnect from reality, we lead them to delusion (stories they tell themselves - rationalization), robbing from them the ability to grow as a person (can't grow if you've already won), and the instilling the misconception that losing is quitting, when in fact it's the opposite - losing is learning.

Setting false beliefs about success can be debilitating. This is not to say we shouldn't help them, praise them, and high-five them for effort. Encouragement and cheerleading is not the same as rewarding. Making sure our kids know that they have everything it takes to win is no doubt part of our charter. It's the gentle push of confidence that helps them realize that they *can* succeed if they do what it takes.

The challenge comes when we over-reward for underperformance. This creates a dissonance that doesn't reveal itself until later in life. When we reward them for just showing up, regardless of ultimate preparation and effort, we instill a sense of victory into a necessary but not sufficient condition to truly winning in life. In other words, our kids equate showing up and smiling with success, shortcutting the true means to *real* success.

> I FAILED OVER AND OVER AGAIN IN MY LIFE AND THAT IS WHY I SUCCEED.
> MICHAEL JORDAN

Then our kids go into the real world. They show up, smile, and someone else passes them by for the victory: money, career, happiness, success, relationships. When the incongruence hits them enough times, our kids are left devastated and distraught. They now have to reconcile that disconnect and either come to the realization that they were misled or develop the delusion that their role in life is that of the victim. Neither one is a great option though it is the latter where we find ourselves most often and at the greatest risk.

Delusion is the separation of our minds from reality. It's the story we tell ourselves so that we can sleep at night even knowing deep down that we're not doing what needs to be done to have that which we want to have. The delusion here is that since we're not winning just by showing up, then someone or something else must be stopping us. We could be the victim of the economy, our boss, our spouse, the government, or just that evil rich guy who has his thumb on us. This is the exact lullaby that will keep us broke and struggling until we are too old to fix it. At that point, reality hits the hardest and we're done. Literally, done.

Over-rewarding also robs our kids of the sting of defeat and the opportunity to improve. After all, if their reward is commensurate with that of the winner, aren't they good enough? What needs to be improved? First, the sting of defeat is not a good feeling. It hurts, it embarrasses, and it demoralizes. This is where our job as parents is crucial. We must show them how to convert the fertilizer of frustration into the fruits of fortune. That hurt should become a seed of mental toughness, the embarrassment a sense of pride in at least competing, and the demoralization a burning desire to do better next time.

Imagine we were to hold and carry around our kids until they were 18 years old, protecting them from the struggle of learning to walk. They would likely be forever crippled. Consider how cruel that would be. Now take this not-so-extreme concept and apply it to anything else we'd like our kids to learn.

Protecting them from defeat through false accomplishment never gives them the chance to learn, grow, and become the person worthy of success. What if we could let them fail in a safe environment, offering the encouragement to get back on the horse with a plan to further develop the necessary skills to do better next time?

THE DIFFERENCE BETWEEN WINNIN AND LOSING IS MOST OFTEN...NOT QUITTING.
WALT DISNEY

We then set the final trap. We tell them L-O-S-E is a four-letter word. And it is, just not that kind. There's a different four-letter word much more worthy of our disgust: Q-U-I-T. The former is often confused for the latter, yet they couldn't be further apart.

If they are losing, aren't they necessarily competing, which is the opposite of quitting? How can they quit anything as long as they're losing at it? Losing, treated as a means of learning, is only temporary. Quitting, however, lasts forever. It not only expels success from our lives, it takes a piece of us with it. We're never quite the same as quitting can be as much of a habit as anything else.

Winning isn't everything, but the process of competing is invaluable. Treating losing as a mean of learning (in spite of the pain of losing) is the path to not quitting and eventually succeeding. Protecting their feelings today will set them up for a delusional tomorrow, one that will come crashing down hard and fast. Let's give them a chance by keeping them safe...from a lifetime of struggle.

Raise our Kids

Find a common interest with you kid and find a challenge beyond their current ability. Perhaps a puzzle, video game, or anything that requires persistence and thinking.

Make a pact with your kid to not quit no matter what. Help them out and make it a team effort. Use any and every resource at your disposal to win the challenge.

Raise ourselves

Read
"Tough times don't last, tough people do", by Robert Schuller
                    And
"The obstacle is the way", by Ryan Holiday

9 Stranger danger

This age-old wisdom we pass to our kids has merit. We don't want them being kidnapped, hurt, or otherwise violated. The challenge is the side-effect of this advice. While there are a few weirdos that we all

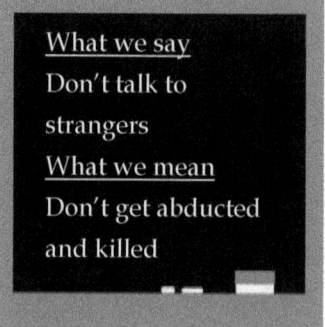

must avoid, most people are just like us: caring, polite human beings that also want the best for them and their family. If you consider that all current friends were once strangers, not talking to them takes on a whole new meaning. In fact, what if not talking to them took on the trappings of a solitary and consequently difficult life?

Human beings are social creatures. Even from a very young age, we have a high propensity to help each other. In his book "Why We Cooperate", Dr. Tomasello points out how infants have the natural inclination to help others that isn't just tied to parents or culture. They instinctively desire to help others, whether it be helping an adult to find something they've lost or another infant to stand. This speaks directly to a principle of nature that we thrive together or die apart. And so we're open to all, without borders or walls.

Somewhere along the way our kids change. We tell our kids to be nice to others but just not to fully trust them. We apply our own insecurities to their behavior and appearance, trying to protect them from any situation where another might think they're different. We want them to fit in; all in an effort to avoid judgement and criticism. Moreover, what will people think of *us* if we have the 'different' kid on the block?

Then it happens. Our kids begin to shirk away and lose their sense of security that they had during the days of running around the house naked in front of company. They begin to see their own value through the eyes of others and start to wonder what other people think about them.

The irony is that nobody is thinking about our kids, rather those people are wondering what *our* kids are thinking about *them*! And so around and around we go following a downward spiral of fear and paranoia of some kind of perverted self-worth. The General Social Survey (GSS) recently found that the number of lonely Americans have tripled in recent decades[6].

IF YOU WANT TO GO FAST, GO ALONE. IF YOU WANT TO GO FAR, GO TOGETHER.

It naturally follows that our kids find an inlet for their loneliness. It helps that we enable them since under our roof, there is protection. There is no need to worry about putting food on the table, paying the light bill, or the mortgage. They can bury themselves into escape activities that either shield them from judgement or make them feel good.

One one hand, there are countless fantasy lands within video games where there is no popularity contest and they can pretend to be the person they wish they were. On the other hand, there is social media that reinforces their need to be liked. It can become so severe that not getting the "like" (hit) and can lead to symptoms not unlike drug withdrawals.

According to a study by RadiumOne, social media usage is a dopamine goldmine (dopamine is our reward neurochemical we feel when we sense

---

[6]https://www.forbes.com/sites/carolinebeaton/2017/02/09/why-millennials-are-lonely/#362b191c7c35

accomplishment)[7]. Our co-dependence on others' opinions is now only a click away.

Soon after, our adulterated kids enter the real world and come to the realization that nobody succeeds alone. That without the ability to elicit help from others, they're doomed to try to succeed on a social island. If they have become immensely dependent on other people's opinions, they find that they cannot operate effectively in public.

They have to join networking groups just to be able to socially interact like a human being. At least in these groups, people are expecting you to share your business and ideas. So at 40 years old, they relearn how to build rapport, make friends, and introduce a business concept without *too* much concern that other folks will find them strange.

Their need for quick acceptance doesn't falter as adults. They are already ingrained and addicted. Few can now endure the withdrawals and their isolation deepens. What's more, their social ineptness creates a host of issues that can manifest itself in some horrific ways. Lack of skills not only produces shyness, but the rejection that comes along with the isolation can create a level of delusion that plays out in violence. Rejection,

---

[7]https://www.ama.org/publications/MarketingNews/Pages/feeding-the-addiction.aspx

bullying, and social isolation are considered key risk factors for school shooters[8].

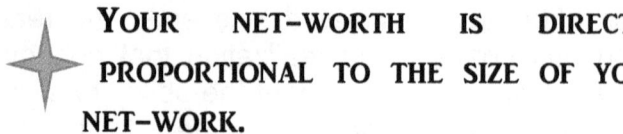

YOUR NET-WORTH IS DIRECTLY PROPORTIONAL TO THE SIZE OF YOUR NET-WORK.

It's no secret that the right social, economic, and political circles have an influence on our success. This doesn't mean they have to pander to any particular group, just that they have the skills to develop those associations that will get them moving on the *right* path.

It's when we start our kids down a path of fear at an early age and then become complicit in the further isolation and degradation of their social skills that puts them in a deficit when having to build trust and key relationships later in life. Let's give them a chance...by helping them develop their social skills, understand the power of helping others, and teaching them how to use the tool of technology responsibly.

---

[8]https://www.valuewalk.com/2018/01/us-school-shootings-causes-solutions/

Raise our Kids

Take a family vacation for one week…from social media and electronic devices. Go somewhere quiet and relaxing and leave all devices at home – cell phones especially included.

Plan the trip to consist of games, campfires, activity, reading, and social outings. Withdrawals should subside after a couple of days.

Raise ourselves

Read
"Speed of Trust", by Stephen M.R. Covey
And
"How to Win Friends and Influence People", by Dale Carnegie

10 Slap a Label

Last time I checked, not one baby arrived in this world with a stamp on their butt saying ""Republican" or "Democrat", "Jewish" or "Hindu", or anything of the sort. They enter the world clean and clear of labels, boxes, and biases. They have an unlimited identity and can be anything they chose.

Eventually they're told and shown that they (well not really they, but us and our family) are of this religion and not those, we always vote for this party, and not that one, and we don't associate with that race/class of people, just these ones.

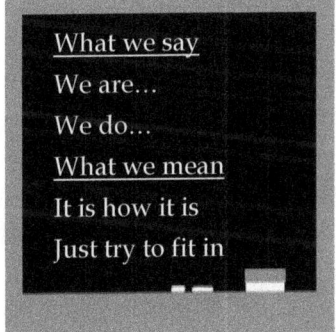

What we say
We are...
We do...
What we mean
It is how it is
Just try to fit in

Then the boxes start forming, the limits start encroaching, and everything needs to be pre-chewed for them. We just can't imagine our kids having to do all this thinking and deciding for themselves only to find out that they would choose differently than us. Not for their sake should they be mistaken in their choice, but for our own validation should we have somehow been duped. Surely our thirty years of existence must be more right than their two years on this planet, right?

Boxes. They're simple, convenient, and many times, wrong. When filling our attic with a bunch of old holiday spirit, it's nice to have neatly labeled boxes so that next year we can easily locate them, decorate our house, and pretend to love each other once again. When we need to prepare our taxes, having a box of receipts and forms is convenient for our accountant. Isn't organization of physical things great?

But when we put anything in boxes that don't physically fit and label them, we almost never get it right, for each label ends up being a generalized opinion that we learned from others or formed through experience, with the former ironically being the most prevalent.

> **LABELS ARE FOR CLOTHING. LABELS ARE NOT FOR PEOPLE.**
> MARTINA NAVRATILOVA

It goes something like this: (All) <blank> are/have/want... It could be philosophical, like priests are good people, or blondes have more fun. It could be political like Republicans want to give tax breaks to the rich or government wants to control us. Whether any of these are true is not the point. It's when we gift these boxes to our kids that we rob them of critical thinking, experience, and ultimately the freedom to choose.

We all know kids are like sponges and while young, we are the authority. Our word is gold. Yet, haven't we formed our own biases over the years from experience, marketing, schooling, and those around us? Even those things that were once true when we were young may have changed faster than our opinion of them.

There was a time when a person could get a four-year degree with no debt and obtain a safe and secure job until retirement, which was funded by a pension that paid us a guaranteed salary until we die. While not impossible to find today, such a scenario is extremely rare, yet the prevailing wisdom from most parents to their kids is to go to school, get a good job, and you're set. To make it worse, we're even taking our own advice at 40 years old, knowing the elevated risk of it not working out.

What boxes and biases are we downloading to them? What if we're passing down 80 year old data and expecting them to win in a society that's moving at the speed of information? Furthermore, imagine the limitations inherent in putting walls around our kids' perception. Every box has a lid, whether inherent or apparent. If our child inherits from us that school is the way to win in life, why should they explore other options? Even though we're in student debt to our eyeballs, they see school as the golden ticket, blinding them to both an alternate option as well as the cost of their decision (what is the ROI on that education - is it worth it?)

In no way am I suggesting school is a bad deal, just that perhaps there could be a drop more thought into whether it is the appropriate vehicle for what our kids want to accomplish in life. What sound family or business *shouldn't* operate looking at cost vs. benefit of any important decision?

> **IT IS BETTER TO DEBATE A QUESTION WITHOUT SETTLING IT THAN TO SETTLE A QUESTION WITHOUT DEBATING IT.**
> JOSEPH JOUBERT

It's understandable to a degree that we try to simplify things for our kids. Like a bird to its offspring, we try to pre-digest what they consume. After all, it's how we as society make it through the day. Sound bites, snippets, and 15 second videos is a big part of our social and news media diet. Somehow we have come to believe our kids as not-so-smart instead of simply inexperienced, confusing intelligence for knowledge. Yet doesn't the former allows for the application of the latter, both critical to our advancement as a society?

So we forget about explaining the complexities of religion or politics to our kids, and we just slap a label on it. Instead of having civil discourse with them, we use insult and assume it isn't worthy of discussion. While doing so prevents confusion, it also prevents critical thinking. It simplifies but also dumbs it down. It offers external clarity while hiding the truth inside. At some point, shouldn't we let our kids "cut their teeth" on some meat and veggies? When should we put away the blender and let them process information for themselves?

As our kids transition to adulthood, it doesn't get easier. Not only do they have a perception of the world that may or may not be consistent with reality, but these barriers and limits have planted the seeds of conflict. Conflict is what happens when we identify with a label. In other words, if we're Republican, that means we're not Democrat. If we're Christian, then we're certainly not Jewish. It's now an *us-versus-them* mentality and if a victor must be chosen, it damn well be us. Nevermind that we may be 99% the same in character, belief, integrity, and moral compass, it only takes one difference to separate an otherwise harmonious existence.

Our kids, having been slapped with a multitude of labels and biases from us, many of which have likely stuck, now struggle to coexist with other groups. This leads to a case of the -isms (racism, sexism, nationalism, populism, etc.) and when they spend more time battling others than building others, they better be at the top of the food chain else they'll be at the bottom with the rest of us.

Finally, they say all good things must come to an end. I disagree and would furthermore amend it to read, "All delusions and falsehoods must come to an end." What happens when their faith is shaken? When their full-scale model of life falls apart because something has woken them up? It takes only one example, incongruent with their labeled perception, to start rocking the boat. It might be what they were told about money, Asians, business, marriage, or even broccoli. The thing is, it's all in the same body of water. When one capsizes, it makes waves for all others.

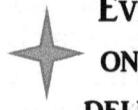 **EVERY PERSON MAKES MISTAKES, BUT ONLY A FOOL PERSISTS IN HIS DELUSIONS.** MARCUS CICERO

If I had a nickel for every time I heard someone proclaim, "I wish I would have known this 20 years ago", I could have bought an island (like Australia) and funded the cure for cancer.

What happens when our kids reach age 65 and they can't retire even though they did exactly what they were told to do (I was a shoestring away from remaining on this path the next 30 years). Who's going to take the mea culpa, us? Maybe society, school, the financial industry? Of course it will be them, but at that point does it matter? They're older, broker, and would give every ounce of their being to be young again.

Consider that our job isn't to replicate ourselves, rather to help them grow into outstanding kids. We are having/had our turn and I hope we've maxed it out and made the most of it. If we have, kudos to us but we must remember times have changed so it may no longer be the way. If we haven't maxed out, haven't even scratched the surface of our potential, how dare we pass that legacy onto our children? For the sake of all that is holy, let's give them a chance...to create their own beliefs and build betterment instead of biases.

Raise our Kids

Use labels to their advantage. Right before you tell them you love them each night, tell them that they're champs, winners, and superstars.

If that's the last thing they hear before closing their eyes every night, they just might start believing it above all else.

Raise ourselves

Read
"What to say when you talk to yourself", by Shad Helmstetter
And
"The Power of the Subconscious Mind", by Joseph Murphy

11  Line Up!

Keep it in the lines. This is generally good advice when using a coloring book or driving a car. In both cases, lines are there for a reason. They help us achieve an objective, like making a picture or traveling somewhere safely. Our kids, however, are born without lines. Their view of the world is blurred and boundaries don't exist.

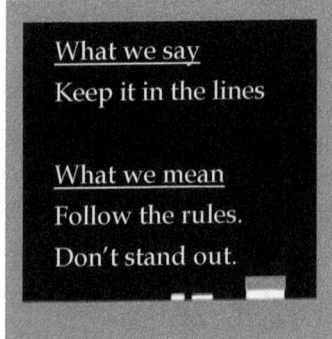

What we say
Keep it in the lines

What we mean
Follow the rules.
Don't stand out.

Naturally, we cannot accept that nature had a higher purpose here. So over the years we train them to focus on the boundaries around them (real or not), forsake creativity for rules, reduce the curiosity that has been fueling them to a pile of local truths (true or not), and stifle their ability to take risks and receive the resultant rewards.

Kids are born with a bounty of creativity. The world is their canvas until we take out our Sharpie and draw the map of life as we see it. Prior to the coloring book, they had to draw the lines to create the picture. Prior to being schooled and given the answers, they had to first ask the questions before they could find the answers, either within or in the outside world. And before we gave them the blinking lights and buzzing ears of social media, they had to invent new ways to spend time with friends, building relationships through mischief and merriment.

ART IS A LIE THAT MAKES US REALIZE THE TRUTH. PABLO PICASSO

We know that creativity is a prerequisite to solving many problems. Albert Einstein has said that our problems cannot be solved at the level of thinking we were at when we created them. This simply means we must grow beyond them and create that which didn't previously exist. Entrepreneurs and business owners must be in a constant state of creation in order to build their dream. Even in corporate America, having the creativity to solve problems is often part of the ladder of success.

Killing creativity isn't hard and we do it to our kids swiftly and efficiently. First we instruct them on exactly what to do and how to do it. These are called rules and that's the way it is in our house. Rules don't need reasons, they just need to be. As kids are essentially our indentured servants, they learn to obey. The consequence of disobeying is punishment and kids generally don't want to do any hard time(out). So they take their ounce of creativity and pour it out into the well of resignation. Eventually, they run out and become what we like to call *well-behaved.* This is not an admonishment of good behavior, but must it be at the expense of creativity?

YOU ARE REMEMBERED FOR THE RULES YOU BREAK. GEN. DOUGLAS MACARTHUR

When they become adults, if they're lucky, they will find out that rules are meant to be followed until broken. They will learn that the wealthiest are the ones that broke the arbitrary rules anyways.

Rules can be very deceiving. Sometimes they are there to protect us or others, yet many times they are there as a show of authority. If nothing else, rules make us feel important since we're probably not getting that level of significance, fulfilment, and appreciation from our job; at least we can be the boss somewhere! Of course, what is that ego costing our kids?

Curiosity may have killed the cat, but lack of it is killing our kids. The most powerful question in the universe is "Why?" It is what propels humankind into action and invention. Without that question, there is not only no progress, there is no *need* to progress. "Why?" is the question that give us the reason to get out of bed in the morning.

Of course, parents would rather avoid such a question, not just because we're tired but often because we don't know. The irony is that we've stopped growing ourselves right around the same age as we deny our kids the chance to learn. According to RQI, question-asking peaks at ages 4 and 5 and then steadily declines immediately after that as answers become more important than questions during their schooling[9].

Kids are also famous for taking risks. They climb trees (or roofs), eat the inedible, and swim in dirty ponds. You know, all those things we wouldn't dare do as an adult. So off they go exploring, learning, and pushing the limits until we scare them with the potential consequences. Certainly a stern warning is prudent with respect to jumping off a bridge and sticking their tongue into an electrical socket.

It's when these warnings become habitual around much lesser things that we throw up yet another set of barriers. Ironically, we often don't speak from experience, rather someone we know, something we read, or our own childhood memories. Regardless, we pass this borrowed "wisdom" to our kids just as their curiosity passes out the window.

---

[9] **http://rightquestion.org/percentage-children-asking-questions/**

YOU DON'T LEARN TO WALK BY FOLLOWING RULES. YOU LEARN BY DOING AND FALLING OVER. RICHARD BRANSON

Something special happens when they take a risk and don't kill themselves doing it. They get a reward. They may receive the delight of creating something, be it a physical object or just a new feeling. Such creations often build confidence and self-worth, for it they can do *that*, what can't they do? Or they may learn that they don't like it. Worst case, they know for a fact to never do it again. Regardless of outcome, they now own it. It is theirs to use the rest of their lives. It's not borrowed from someone else, rather an experience that could never have been taught. The best lessons are never taught, they can only be caught.

When left to their own devices, kids will push the boundaries around them through curiosity and risk-taking. Outside of doing anything that could severely injure them, what would be the harm in allowing them to explore? Sure, they may come to the same roadblock we do and then they'll know firsthand that it's time to stop. On the other hand, such a roadblock may inspire a dose of creativity that nobody before had considered.

What if the size of their success will be tied to the size of the problem they solve? Should we not allow them the benefits of this failure/learning process, we will assuredly drain whatever energy, creativity, and faith in themselves that's left. Let's encourage our kids' creativity and let them out of the lines as much as possible.

Raise our Kids

Have your kid *create* art. Art could be paint, clay, pencil, music, writing, dance, etc. Let them express themselves in something without borders. No judgement. It's not for you to understand, it's for them to share.

When they are happy with their creation, find a way to publish it. Use newspaper, paperback, website, social media, or any other means to get it out to the public.

Raise ourselves

Read
"Unlimited Power", by Tony Robbins
And
"Screw it, let's do it.", by Sir Richard Branson

12 Bad Copy

This is a personal not-so-favorite of mine as it was drilled into my psyche almost every day of my childhood. While what we say has immense power when repeated ad infinitum, at the end of the day, what we *do*

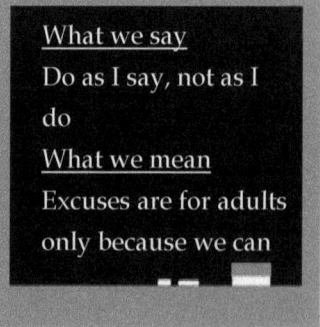

What we say
Do as I say, not as I do
What we mean
Excuses are for adults only because we can

becomes the most influential role model for our kids.

They say our kids' ears are closed to what we say but are wide open to what we do. What if we are not only replicating our substandard lives into our kids but in trying to cover up our shortcomings, we set the perfect example on how best to make excuses, ignore the truth, and give up on life's most precious offering: growth?

If there's one thing we typically do right, it's that we don't let our kids hang out with the wrong crowd. We know without doubt that if they associate with drug dealers, criminals, pimps, or gamblers, it is only a matter of time before the police come knocking on our doors with the bad news. So we shield them and protect them from poor outside influence, but what about their closest inside associations of school, marketing, and of course, family? What example are we setting for our kids? Who are *we* hanging out with?

They hear to save money, but they see us spending like crazy, going into mountains of debt that will take five lifetimes to pay off, and then stressing about it. They hear to eat healthy vegetables and clean protein but they see us eating out, engorging on fast food because we're in a rush, only to be fed a quick mac-n-cheese at home - the definition of nutrition-less.

They hear to respect others and make friends but see us fighting with our spouses, fighting within political circles, and fighting with our boss to eke out a cost-of-living raise so that we don't have to tap into our overextended home equity line of credit.

They hear to read a book and study hard but they see us get home from the job we abhor and sit down to watch four hours of television or stare into our phones in a desperate attempt to forget about our broke, unhealthy, stressful lives.

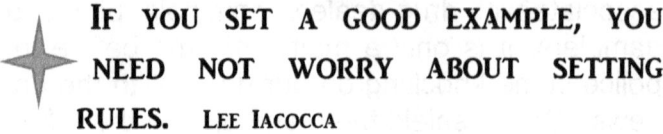

> **IF YOU SET A GOOD EXAMPLE, YOU NEED NOT WORRY ABOUT SETTING RULES.** LEE IACOCCA

If our kids take our lead and do what we do, then time will tell if it was the right thing. If it isn't, one would expect that there may be a wake-up call or two along the way. After all, nobody becomes broke, obese, or unhappy overnight. It takes years if not decades to destroy all that nature has gifted us.

Consider that the vast majority of people earn well over $1M in their working lifetime (even high school dropouts)[10], how is that there's little to nothing to show for it? At what point do we wake up and find that we're just one more cheeseburger away from a heart attack or stroke? How many fruitless hours at a job in which we're underpaid and underappreciated does it take to build up to our current level of unhappiness and lack of fulfilment?

One of the clearest examples of a bad copy is how our kids eat. Every meal is about pleasure and

---

[10] **https://www.census.gov/prod/2012pubs/acsbr11-04.pdf**

nutrition happens by accident, if at all. What we don't always consider is how poor nutrition leads to poor energy, poor habits, and poor everything else. If the fuel is bad, nothing else can work properly. No matter how we wish to delude ourselves, kids don't naturally eat garbage food because garbage food isn't natural. Imagine what would happen long-term if we set a better example for them.

What's worse, as we tell our kids one thing and show them another, we teach them the power of excuses. Excuses are the little bridges of rationalization between what we say and why we do. It's one of the most powerful inoculations to winning in life.

Excuses are different than reasons. A reason is why something is the way it is whereas an excuse is how we blame something else and ultimately give up our responsibility for it. For example, if we're wet from rain, the excuse is to blame the weather, but the reason is because we went outside without an umbrella. Excuses allow us to do one thing and blame someone else when it doesn't work out. How cruel is it then to pass this devilish inheritance on to our young ones?

HE THAT IS GOOD AT MAKING EXCUSES IS SELDOM GOOD FOR ANYTHING ELSE.
BEN FRANKLIN

So the wakeup call arrives (more often than they realize) and our kids politely excuse it away. Moreover, their associations reinforce this behavior. As younger children, it's us as parents that show the way to Excuseville. As they get older, the schools do very well to ensure that any substandard performance is first politically and correctly excused away before considering that they may just need a good boot in the butt. And from start to finish, marketing and advertising convince them that nothing is their fault and that the way to fix their ills is to buy this product, eat this stuff, take out this loan, or if all else fails, drink more beer.

What happens when they become adults and nobody is watching over them anymore? Who monitors their associations then? What happens when all the success-killing things they've done that were excused away finally catch up with reality? Unfortunately, once the habits of poor associations and excuse-making are built, there may be no escape until the day of reckoning when the consequences of all their actions comes to a head.

At the end of the day, when our kids become us in almost every way, why is it that we're surprised, offended, and disheartened? At what point did we really expect our kids to suddenly figure out that which we didn't know, couldn't teach, and never shared? Again, no judgement on who they are or what they do, but the only surprising thing is that we're surprised.

Imagine forgetting that we're old, it's too late, or that we can't setting the bar by our actions instead of through empty words. Let's give our kids a chance... by showing them so clearly that words aren't necessary.

Raise our Kids

Write down three things that you wish to see improved in your kid. Choose at least one and write a plan on how to improve that area _**in yourself.**_

Share it with your family and let them know what you are changing, how you are changing, and why you wish to improve. Be honest.

Write the plan and follow it to the letter. Remember that your child is watching and will pick up on and copy your habits – new or old.

Raise ourselves

Read
"Eat that frog", by Brian Tracy
               And
"The compound effect", by Darren Hardy

13 CHiLdiSH SucceSS

The real lesson here is that there is so much we can learn from our kids. Perhaps our kids should be raising us instead of us lowering them! What if we got back to nature, to the source that provided us with winning ways before we became adulterated?

Before you dismiss it as an exercise in futility, consider that most successful people just forgot how to "grow up" in one way or another. They never quite got with the rules either through lack of understanding or defiance. Ironically, society doesn't put up very well with these two traits in our kids.

The thing is that kids are born to win, conditioned to lose. As adults, we are just conditioned and trained kids with a bigger shoe size. What traits to kids have that we can use to rekindle our childish ways and turn them into successful habits?

Childish Traits

1. **Have a sense of urgency.** Good things come to those who hustle. You don't have as much time as you think. Getting it done faster not only gets it done, but frees you to follow other and bigger passions.

2. **Focus on your vision.** If you don't know where you're going, every road will take you nowhere. It's not a matter of being somewhere in the future, just where will it be and will it be where you had hoped. Be clear about it.

3. **Keep a positive attitude.** Winning is hard enough, why start off in a deficit? Having a poor attitude is a surefire way to create poor behavior and undesirable results. Have gratitude for where you are and a smile for what's to come.

4. **Stay curious.** Ask the right questions and seek to understand everything important. Seek out advice from experts, not family. Microphones don't make people right, just loud. Ask, ask, ask.

5. **Be creative.** Actually, we are always creating – whether it be bad things or good things. Find ways to express your creativity and don't worry about what others think. They're not Olympic judges and they're not paying your bills. Go for it.

6. **Start liking money.** Forget any belief about money that doesn't serve you to earn more in a moral, ethical and legal way. Also do no listen to broke people on how to be wealthy. That is another antidote to wealth.

7. **Take risks.** Don't do anything physically or financially foolish, but on those things where a loss won't actually kill you, say YES. Before you think about the worst thing that could happen, consider the best thing that could happen and choose the upside as often as you can.

8. **Build faith.** Recognize and celebrate small successes. *You* must believe in you before anyone else will. Start everything with success as the assumption.

9. **Stop hating.** Hating of any kind is a venomous trap. It's like drinking poison hoping the other person dies. If you were wronged, forgive anyways since it's really the best give you can give yourself

10. **Enjoy socializing.** Get to genuinely know and care about others. See everyone as a valuable person in their own right. You are only one solid association from meeting the person that will change your life forever. Besides, we win together or we lose together.

11. **Fight hard.** Fight for what you want. Work hard and if need be work harder. As long as you're working on the right things, success is inevitable. Like a child wanting a cookie, get clever and be persistent.

12. **Never give up.** Never ever. Most people stop inches before the goal. If you're going to pay the price, you might as well get the reward. Giving up is the only way to fail.

Go to
www.lifesaverLD.org/adulterated

There you will be able to download the official Childish Challenge along with a 3 month calendar to rekindle your youthful ways. It might even actually make you younger!

14 Give 'em a chance

It's never a simple task to lead others, especially those that start life so innocent and incompetent. Then again, isn't that what makes it worth it? That one day they will exceed our limits and expectations? This is highly unlikely to happen without a conscious effort to become leaders in our own family. To lead their curiosity, energy, friendliness, competitiveness, and mindset towards becoming the person worthy of all their hopes and dreams.

It's no coincidence that many world leaders are on the mature and wiser side. Surely young folks can start the process of becoming a great leader and even show signs of wisdom not commonly found in youth. It's just that experience is the best teacher which makes our job as their leaders that much more important. We all must learn how to be a good follower in order to be a great leader, so let's give them a chance.

Though not a discussion for this book, it's worth mentioning that it used to take a village to raise a child for the reasons above. There were elders whose wisdom in these areas were heeded. We've transitioned over many years to raising our direct offspring as if they were our possession alone, and not that of the greater community. While legally that may be true, the results of what we raise are indeed the concern of society as a whole. At the end of the day, donating DNA to a child does not make us any more qualified to raise that child than buying an airplane makes us qualified to fly it. Parenting is a skill, not a title or a position you would get in a job. It's a verb that requires action, planning, and oftentimes a new mindset. Instead of expecting a newly-conditioned 20 year old to properly raise a child, let's give them a chance.

Is this book suggesting we give a license to our kids to run free without discipline? No. There can and should be a balance between discipline and rules with creativity and expression of energy. They can think big while focusing on the small things. They must find the coexistence of being competitive with that of kind and helpful. They should learn to control their gifts without subduing or giving up on them.

Let's set the pace. As society, let's show them the power of cooperation. As a school system, let's allow them to express the crazy while learning the laws of our universe. As parents, let's show them, not tell them, how to win in life. Let's all equip them with the tools, mindset, and toughness to give them a fighting chance to become the best version of themselves.

Godspeed!

www.ingramcontent.com/pod-product-compliance
Lightning Source LLC
Chambersburg PA
CBHW060203050426
42446CB00013B/2971